EXCEL VBA:

A BEGINNERS' GUIDE

RAJAN

Contents at a Glance

Acknowledgement

I would like to express my gratitude to my friends and family who made their contribution to the successful publication of this book.

My special thanks to my family, friends and colleagues. I would like to thank my readers for their constant support and encouragement.

Disclaimer

This book is an independent publication and it does not affiliate or sponsored by Microsoft Corporation.

1) Introduction to Excel VBA

VBA abbreviation is Visual Basic for Applications. It is not a completely object oriented language instead we can say it as event driven programming language because to run your script you need a host. Microsoft Office comes with inbuilt Visual basic Editor to write your code easily. Using the power of VBA you can easily able to access the COM objects of all Microsoft office. For instance, you can open new word document using excel VBA, you can send the all details of your excel sheet to word document, you can control Microsoft outlook using VBA.

But among the Microsoft programs, VBA for Excel is most popular used application because almost all kinds of works are done in Excel when compared to other programs such as Outlook, Power point, Access. So, if you know VBA for excel then you can easily do almost all your stuff without any hassle.

Microsoft Excel by default comes with thousands of inbuilt functions. Even though it has many functions, it does not satisfy all the users' requirement. In order to resolve this problem, Microsoft allows user to create their own functions according to their requirement with the help of VBA.

For example, if you want to convert the degree to Celsius or Fahrenheit using Excel built in functions is complex, but it is relatively easy to solve this problem by creating your own function using VBA.

Visual Basic for Application allow user to create customized User Defined Functions, automating the manual process ,controlling the windows AP.VBA is somewhat closely related to Visual basic but it need a host application to run your code. You cannot able to create a standalone application using VBA.

VBA is built into most of the Microsoft Office Applications to allow the user to meet their requirements. It interacts with other application using the OLE automation technology. Sometime VBA can also be called as Macro.

To start writing your script you need to have the Developer tab but by default Developer tab is hidden by Microsoft. You need to activate it. Let us see how to activate the Developer tab. The screenshots attached in the book is Microsoft Excel 2007 the appearance may look different in other versions but the code will be compatible with all Excel versions.

Click on the Excel Office button and choose the Excel options then the dialog box will appear as show in the Fig 1.1.Mark the check box "Show Developer tab in the Ribbon" and click the ok button then you can able to see the Developer tab added to your Excel as shown in the Fig 1.2

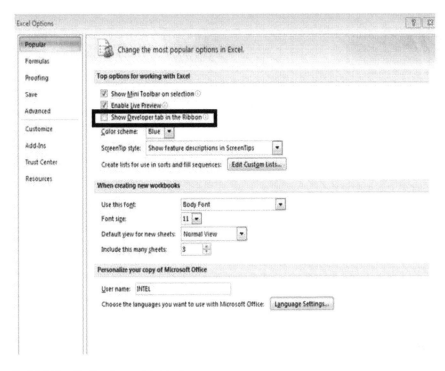

Fig 1.1 Adding the Developer tab to Excel

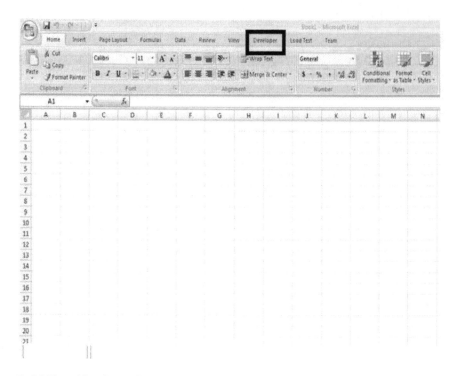

Fig 1.2 After adding the Developer tab to Excel

Navigate to the developer tab to explore the options available in the tab.

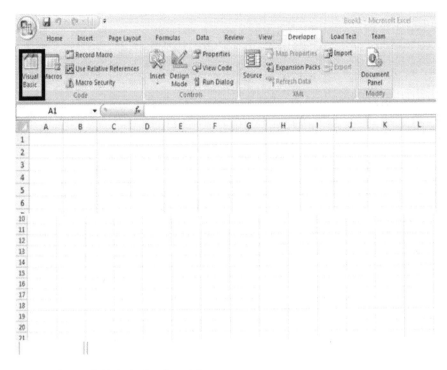

Fig 1.3 Options available in the Developer tab

To write your first script we need to open the Visual Basic Editor and to do that click on the Visual Basic button as shown in the Fig 1.3.You can able to see the Visual Basic Editor window appear on the screen.

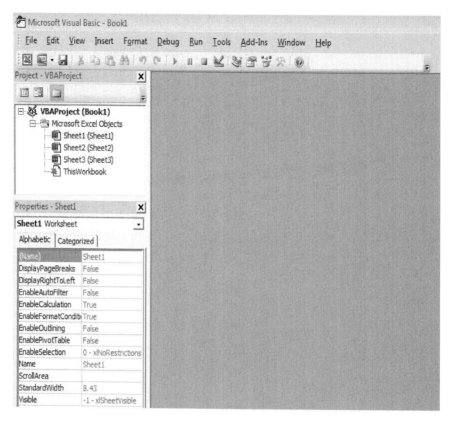

Fig 1.4 Visual Basic Editor Window

Till now we are not ready to write our code because we need to insert a module to write our code. To do those in the Visual Basic Editor window click Insert ->Module. After that you can able to see the window similar to the below Fig 1.5

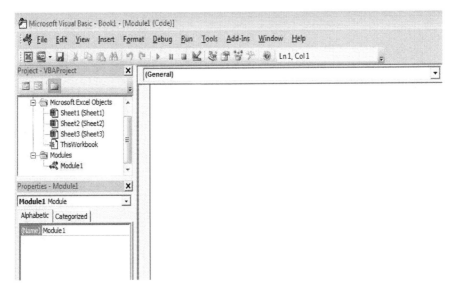

Fig 1.5 After inserting the Module to VB Editor

Now we will do simple thing like addition and subtractions.

Below are the steps we are going to do using the VBA code

Step 1: Assigning "A1" to 5

Step 2: Assigning "B1" to 7

Step 3: Adding "A1" and "B1" and display its value in the "C1"

Step 4: Assigning "A2" to 10

Step 5: Assigning "B2" to 15

Step 6: Subtracting the value "A2" from "B2"

Step 7: Displaying the subtracted value in the "C2"

It may look somewhat complicate but it's very easy once you are comfortable with VBA

As I previously mentioned our codes are stored as module in the VBA so first thing we need to do is to create a subroutine named "calc". Sub routines are procedures which contain our macro. Below is the syntax for subroutine

Sub <**Procedure Name**>()

Your code goes here

End Sub

Our macro lies within the subroutine named "Calc"

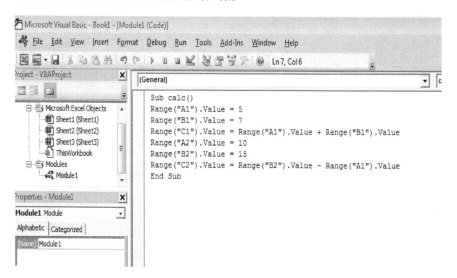

Fig 1.6 Code for addition and subtraction

Range("A1").value=5 It assigns the value 5 to the cell "A1".Be cautious that it will assign the value 5 to the currently active sheet. Suppose if the active sheet of your Excel workbook is Sheet 3 then it will enter the value 5 in the sheet 3 not in the sheet 1

Note:If you want the value 5 to be appear in the sheet 1 then you can specify that properly in your code like the below statement

Sheets(1).Range("A1").Value = 5

The above statement enters the value 5 only in the sheet 1 irrespective of which sheet is currently active in your workbook.

Like other programming language you can use the Arithmetic operations in VBA.

Range("C1").Value = Range("A1").Value + Range("B1").Value This statement first add the value of "A1" and "B1" assign the total to the value "C1"

Do the same for subtraction.

To run the code Press F5 or Go to Run->Run sub/Userform in the VBA editor window. Output will be displayed in the sheet1 in excel if sheet 1 is active sheet.

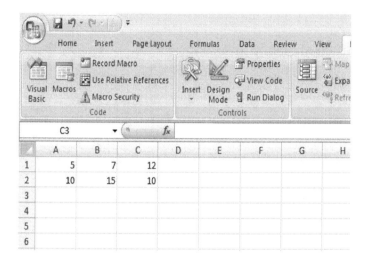

Fig1.7 Output of our code

2) Declaring Variables

Variables are the storage location of your values in the computer memory.VBA allow the user to store different type of Data such as Boolean(true or false), string, numbers, double(precision values) etc.

VBA has certain rules to accept your variable name. Below are the rules you need to follow for your variable name

1) The length of the variable must be less than 255 characters

2) Space or periods are not allowed

3) Special characters like (#, $, %, &,!) is not acceptable

4) First character must not be numeric

How to declare a variable?

Variable should be declared with Dim(Optional) statement as prefix and followed by its datatype (optional).If variable don't have a datatype like string, integer then VBA assigned default data type called Variant. Data stored as Variant acts like chameleon and it changes its type according to the value you assigned to the variable.

Example 2.1

Dim firstval as integer

Dim firstname as string

Dim bday as Date

Dim isit as boolean

In general, VBA datatypes are divided into two types. They are

1)Numeric data types

2)Non numeric data types

1)Numeric data types

Numeric data types are used to deals with different numerical format such as decimals, fractions, integers etc. Below are the list of numeric data types, space it allocates to store the value and the range of values it can handle.

Data Types	Byte Used	Range of Values
Integer	2 Bytes	−32,768 to 32,767
Long	4 Bytes	−2,147,483,648 to 2,147,483,647
Single	4 Bytes	−3.402823E38 to −1.401298E-45 (for negative values);
Double	8 Bytes	−1.79769313486232E308 to −4.94065645841247E-324 (negative values); 4.94065645841247E-324 to
Decimal	12 Bytes	/−79,228,162,514,264,337,593,543,950,335 with no decimal point; +/−7.9228162514264337593543950335 with 28 places to the right of the decimal
Currency	8 Bytes	−922,337,203,685,477.5808 to 922337203685477

Example 2.2

Dim a as Integer

a=99999

When you declare a above statements you can able to assign only values in the range −32,768 to 32,767 suppose if you try to assign greater value(a=99999) than the range then it will throw overflow error message as shown below

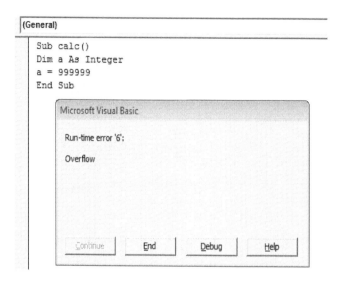

Fig 2.1 Overflow error message

Before choosing the data types ensure that your value is within the range of chosen data type. Otherwise it will display the above error message during the run time. To debug the above code you need to declare a data type as long, single or double.

2)Non Numeric Data Types

Non Numeric data types are used to deals with non numerical data such as byte, logical values (true or false), date, string (text) etc. Below are the list of non-numeric data types, space it allocates to store the value and the range of values it can handle

Data Types	Byte Used	Range of Values
Byte	1 byte	0 to 255
Boolean	2 bytes	True or False
Date	8 bytes	January 1, 0100 to December 31, 9999
Object	4 bytes	Any object reference
String(Variable length)	10 bytes + string length	0 to approximately 2 billion characters
String(Fixed length)	Length of string	1 to approximately 65,400 characters
Variant(with numbers)	16 bytes	Any numeric value up to the range of a double data type. It can also hold special values, such as Empty, Error, Nothing, and Null.
Variant(with characters)	22 bytes + string length	0 to approximately 2 billion
User defined	Varies	Varies by element

Example 2.3

Dim name as string

name="John"

The first statement declare a variable called name with data type as string and the second statement assign the string "John" to the variable. So, whenever you use its variable name "name" it contain its value "John".

Example 2.4

Dim bday as Date

bday="12/01/1999"

First statement declares a variable bday with data type as Date and second statement assign the "12/01/1999" to the variable named bday.

Example 2.5

We will see another example for declaring a variable,assigning value to the variable and showing that value in the excel sheet

```
Sub calc()
'Declaring variables
Dim a As Integer
Dim b As Long
Dim c As Single
Dim d As Double
Dim e As Byte
Dim f As Boolean
Dim g As Date
Dim h
'Assigning value to the variables
a = 9999
b = 569875
c = 3.402823E+38
d = 1.69769313486232E+308
e = 125
f = True
g = "January 01 1992"
h = "12128hello"
'Displaying in the excel sheet
Range("A1").Value = a
Range("B1").Value = b
Range("C1").Value = c
Range("D1").Value = d
Range("E1").Value = e
Range("F1").Value = f
Range("G1").Value = g
Range("H1").Value = h
End Sub
```

Fig 2.2 Example for declaring, assigning and displaying the value in the excel sheet

Use of Option Explicit

The best way to write your program is to declare a variable first before using that but VBA doesn't ask you to declare a variable unless you use a command called "Option Explicit"

When VBA detects the **option explicit** commands then it will search for variable which is not declared and throw an error message to declare a variable. Option Explicit command should be used outside the sub routine command.

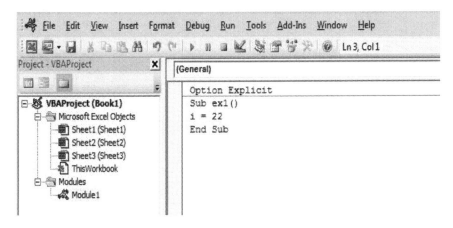

Fig 2.3 Use of option explicit

In the Fig 2.3, you can find the Option explicit command in the top and variable 'i' assigned with value 22 without Dim statement. When executing it compiler throws an error message as "Variable not defined". It is always best practice to use the Option Explicit command to avoid run time error and duplicate of variable.

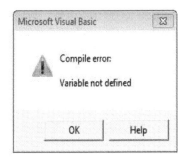

Fig 2.4 Compiler error message

3) Working with Ranges

Range object is used to represent cell or group of cells in the worksheet. It is one of the most important objects in VBA. We will see a various examples related to Ranges

Example 3.1

Assigning a value to the Range "A1"

Range("A1").Value = 5

Statement is simple and we already familiar with this and it's just assign a value 5 to the cell "A1"

Example 3.2

Assigning a value to group of cells

Range("A1:B5").value="Hello"

It assigns the value "Hello" to the Range("A1:B5")

	A	B	C
1	Hello	Hello	
2	Hello	Hello	
3	Hello	Hello	
4	Hello	Hello	
5	Hello	Hello	
6			

Fig 3.1 Output of Example 3.2

Example 3.3

Copying a value from one cell to another cell

Range("A1").Copy Range("B1")

It copies the value from the cell "A1" and paste the value in the Cell "D2".Ensure that value should exist in the cell "A1" for copying.

Code

```
(General)

Sub rang()
Range("A1").Value = 23
Range("A1").Copy Range("D2")

End Sub
```

Fig 3.2 Copy cell from one range to another range

Output

	A	B	C	D	E
1	23				
2				23	
3					
4					
5					
6					

Fig 3.3 Output for the Example 3.3

Example 3.4

In some cases you need to copy a range of cells to another location but you don't know the exact number of columns and rows in the sheet.

Enter some range of values in the sheet 1

	A	B	C
1	Nam	Emp ID	
2	John	9876	
3	Smith	4563	
4	Henry	9856	
5	Ben	5163	
6			
7			

19

Fig 3.4 Range of cells in sheet 1

Execute the below code

```
Sub rang()

Sheets(1).Range("A1").CurrentRegion.Copy Sheets(2).Range("B2")

End Sub
```

Fig 3.5 Macro for copying the range

The above Macro copy the range of values as shown in the Fig 3.4 from the sheet 1 to sheet 2 in the position "B2". Here, we just gave "B2" and VBA take it as reference and place the remaining values in the corresponding cells.

	A	B	C	D
1				
2		Nam	Emp ID	
3		John	9876	
4		Smith	4563	
5		Henry	9856	
6		Ben	5163	
7				
8				
9				

Fig 3.6 copying the value in the sheet 2

Example 3.5

Now we are going to select a range of cells and changing the properties of it.

```
Sub rang()
Range("A1:B5").Font.Bold = True
Range("A1:B5").Font.Strikethrough = True
End Sub
```

Fig 3.7 changing the properties of Range

It changes the font type of the Range "A1:B5" to bold and strike through.

	A	B	C
1	Nam	Emp ID	
2	John	9876	
3	Smith	4563	
4	Henry	9856	
5	Ben	5163	
6			
7			

Fig 3.8 Output of the macro shown in the Fig 3.7

Example 3.6

Moving a range from one place to another place using the method called cut

```
Sub rang()
Range("A1:B5").Value = "Hi"
Range("A1:B5").Cut Range("C1")
End Sub
```

Fig 3.9 Macro for copying

It assigns the value "Hi "to the range "A1:B5" and when the second statements executed it cut the value from the range "A1:B5" and paste the value to "C1"

The output is shown below

	A	B	C	D
1			Hi	Hi
2			Hi	Hi
3			Hi	Hi
4			Hi	Hi
5			Hi	Hi
6				
7				

Fig 3.10 Output for Example 3.6

Till now, we saw how to refer range by mentioning its Range as A1 or A1:B5 etc. Now let us see, another way of referring the range by its rows and column positions.

How to calculate cell positions?

Cell Positions can be calculated by counting its rows and columns. It's like representation of co-ordinate (x, y) in a graph sheet.

21

Here x represent row and y represent column. But in Microsoft excel x and y is always positive integer.

For example A1 can be represented as (1,1) because it lies in the first row and first column, B3 can be represented as Cells (3, 2) and D5 can be represented as Cells (5, 4).

Exercise for you

Cells (4, 9) represent?

Cells (5, 7) represent?

C10 can be represented as?

E7 can be represented as?

Example 3.7

```
Sub rang()
Sheets(1).Activate
Range(Cells(1, 3), Cells(2, 5)).Value = "Hello world"
End Sub
```

Fig 3.11 Macro by referring the ranges by column and row position numbers

Sheets (1).Activate- This statement make the sheet 1 as active

Range(Cells(1,3),Cells(2,5)).Value ="Hello world"- This statements set the value "Hello world" to

(Cells (start row position, start column position), Cells (Last row position, Last column position))

Cells (1, 3) referring the range "C1"

Cells (2, 5) referring the range "E2"

4)If...Else statements

4.1 If statements

IF statement checks the condition given by the programmer is true or not. If the condition is true then IF statement will execute otherwise the compiler will skip the statement and start compiling the next statement.

Syntax

If <condition> then <instructions>

Example 4.1

```
Sub ifstat()
Dim i As Integer
Dim j As Integer
i = 9
j = 9
If i = j Then Sheets(1).Cells(1, 1) = "If statement executed"
End Sub
```

Fig 4.1 If statement example

The condition (i=j) given in the code compare the value of i and j and if both are equal then it will print the value "If statement executed "in the cell "A1"

Output

	A	B	C
1	If statement executed		
2			
3			
4			
5			
6			

Fig 4.2 output of Ex 4.1

Suppose if you want to enter the instructions part Sheets(1).Cells(1,1)="If statement executed" in the next line then you need to close the if statement with End if statement

Syntax for If...End If statement

If <condition> then

<Instructions>

End If

Example 4.2

```
Sub ifstat()
Dim i As Integer
Dim j As Integer
i = 9
j = 9
If i = j Then
Sheets(1).Cells(1, 1) = "If statement executed"
End If
End Sub
```

Fig 4.3 If End If statement example

The output of the above program is same as output of Ex 4.1

4.2 If then Else Statement

The instruction given in the If statement will be executed only if condition is true otherwise instruction given in the else statement will be executed (If present).

Syntax

If <condition> then

<Instruction>

Else

<Instruction>

End if

Example 4.3

```
Sub ifstat()
Dim i As Integer
Dim j As Integer
i = 9
j = 20
If i = j Then
Sheets(1).Cells(1, 1) = "If statement executed"
Else
Sheets(1).Cells(1, 1) = "Else statement exeucted"
End If
End Sub
```

Fig 4.4 If Else statement

In the above code the condition (i=j) is failed so else statement executed and it will print the output "Else statement executed" in the cell "A1"

4.4 Multiple If else statements

It allow the user to compare single variable with multiple values and if any the condition is true then the instruction corresponding to the condition will be executed otherwise the condition given in the else statement will be executed (If present).

Syntax

If <condition> then

<Instructions>

Elseif<condition> then

<Instructions>

Else

<Instruction> then

End if

Example 4.4

```
Sub ifstat()
Dim i As Integer
Dim j As Integer
i = 9
j = 20
If i = j Then
Sheets(1).Cells(1, 1) = "If statement executed"
ElseIf i = 9 Then
Sheets(1).Cells(1, 1) = "Else if statement exeucted"
Else
Sheets(1).Cells(1, 1) = "Else statement executed"
End If
End Sub
```

Fig 4.5 Multi If else statements

The value of i is 9 given in the second statement met the criteria so the cells (1, 1) shows the value "Else if statement executed"

Output

	A	B	C
1	Else if statement exeucted		
2			
3			
4			
5			
6			
7			

Fig 4.6 Output of Example 4.4

4.5 Nested If statement

Nested if conditions are self-explanatory. It surrounds with Nesting of If else statements and if the condition met then it transfer the control to the inside branch of If statement and where also same rule applicable. This will be helpful if your code need to satisfy nested conditions.
Syntax

If<condition> then

    If<condition> then

<Instruction>

Else

<Instruction>

End if

Else

<Instruction>

End if

Example 4.5

```
Sub ifstat()
Dim i As Integer
Dim j As Integer
i = 9
j = 9
'Nested if statements
If i = j Then

    If i = 9 Then
        Sheets(1).Cells(1, 1) = " Nested If statement executed"
    Else
        Sheets(1).Cells(1, 1) = " Nested If statement not executed"
    End If

Else

Sheets(1).Cells(1, 1) = "Else statement executed"

End If
End Sub
```

Fig 4.7 Nested if statement

The first condition i=j is satisfied so the compiler start compiling the condition in the next line i=9 which is nested inside it. This is also true so, it print the given value and exit both of the if statements

Output

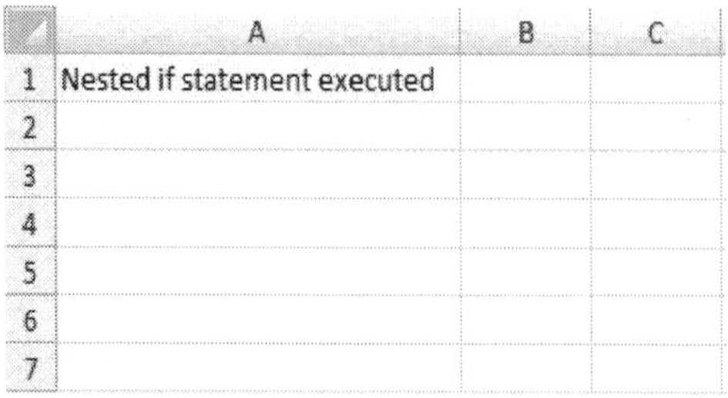

	A	B	C
1	Nested if statement executed		
2			
3			
4			
5			
6			
7			

Fig4.8 Output of Example 4.5

5)Select case statements

Select case statements is best alternative to the If else statements. If your script consists of more number of If else statements or to avoid confusion you can go with select case statements. It will be the best replacement for the If else statements.

In select case statements, given condition compared with multiple cases and if any case matches then the compiler execute the instructions given in that case. Suppose if none of the cases matches then instructions in the **case else** statement will be executed. If no case else statement present and no cases matches with expression then the compiler comes out of the select case statement and start executing the line next to Select case statement

Syntax

*Select case <**Expression or condition**>*

>   *Case<value>*

>   >   *<Instruction>*

>   *Case<value>*

>   >   *<Instruction>*

>   *Case<value>*

>   >   *<Instruction>*

>   *Case<value>*

>   >   *<Instruction>*

>   *Case else*

>   >   *<Instruction>*

End select

Example 5.1

```
Sub selectcase()
Dim b As Integer
b = 35

'Select case statements
Select Case b
    Case 0 To 5
        Sheets(1).Cells(1, 1) = "Case 1 statement executed"
    Case 6 To 10
        Sheets(1).Cells(1, 1) = "Case 2 statement executed"
    Case 11 To 20
        Sheets(1).Cells(1, 1) = "Case 3 statement executed"
    Case 21 To 40
        Sheets(1).Cells(1, 1) = "Case 4 statement executed"
    Case Else
        Sheets(1).Cells(1, 1) = "Case Else statement executed"
End Select

End Sub
```

Fig 5.1 Select case statement

The variable "b" is having value 35. In the select case statement we are comparing the value of b with five different cases and it was fall under the case 21 to 40 so the value of the "A1" will be "Case 4 statement executed"

Output

	A	B	C
1	Case 4 statement executed		
2			
3			
4			
5			
6			
7			

Fig 5.2 output of Fig 5.1

Select case statement using Is keyword

Is keyword is generally used to compare the numeric values using arithmetic operators in the cases with case expression or condition.

Example 5.2

```
Sub selectcase()
Dim b As Integer
b = 35

'Select case statements
Select Case b
    Case Is < 5
        Sheets(1).Cells(1, 1) = "Case 1 statement executed"
    Case Is < 10
        Sheets(1).Cells(1, 1) = "Case 2 statement executed"
    Case Is < 20
        Sheets(1).Cells(1, 1) = "Case 3 statement executed"
    Case Is < 40
        Sheets(1).Cells(1, 1) = "Case 4 statement executed"
    Case Else
        Sheets(1).Cells(1, 1) = "Case Else statement executed"
End Select

End Sub
```

Fig 5.3 Select case with Is keyword

First case compare the value b with 5 to verify the value of b is less than 5, second case verify the value of b is less than 10, third case verify the value of b is less than 20, fourth case verify the value of b is less than 40 and its true so it will print "Case 4 statement executed" in the "A1"

Output

	A	B	C
1	Case 4 statement executed		
2			
3			
4			
5			
6			

Fig 5.4 Output of Fig 5.3

Select case statement with comma delimiter

Comma in the case statement is used to compare the list of values separated by comma in the single case statement with case expression. If any of the values in any of the cases matches with the expression then the instructions given in the corresponding case statement will be executed. This would be helpful when you need to compare some random set of numbers or strings in a single case.

Example 5.3

```
Sub selectcase()
Dim b As Integer
b = 35

'Select case statements
Select Case b
    Case 5, 10
        Sheets(1).Cells(1, 1) = "Case 1 statement executed"
    Case 15, 20
        Sheets(1).Cells(1, 1) = "Case 2 statement executed"
    Case 20, 35
        Sheets(1).Cells(1, 1) = "Case 3 statement executed"
    Case 30, 40
        Sheets(1).Cells(1, 1) = "Case 4 statement executed"
    Case Else
        Sheets(1).Cells(1, 1) = "Case Else statement executed"
End Select

End Sub
```

Fig 5.5 Select case with comma delimiter

In first case the value of b is compared with 5 and 10, second case value of b is compared with 15&20, third case the value of b is compared with 20&35, fourth case the value of b is compared with 30 and 40.But the third case met the condition so it will be executed.

Output

	A	B	C
1	Case 3 statement executed		
2			
3			
4			
5			
6			
7			
8			
9			
10			

Fig 5.6 Output of Fig 5.5

6)For Next statements

For Next is one of the most commonly used loop control in VBA. The use of for loop is to repeat a group of statements for specified number of times.

Syntax

For counter =start value to end (Step value)

> *<Instruction>*

> *<Instruction>*

> *<Exit For>*

> *<Instruction>*

Next counter

Note: Counter is any integer variable

The For loop require the counter start value and end value to repeat the loop for n number of times. Keyword **Step** is optional and using the step you can control the increment value of the counter. **Exit For** is used to terminate the For loop.

6.1 Simple For loop statement

```
Sub forloop()

Dim i As Integer
'For loop
For i = 1 To 10
    Sheets(1).Cells(i, 1).Value = i
Next i

End Sub
```

Fig 6.1 Simple For loop statement

For i=1 to 10 statement inform compiler to iterate the loop for 10 times.

Sheets(1).cells(**i**,1).value= **i** Every time this loop execute variable **i** value differs in both the sides. For example, in the first iteration the value of i is 1 so it refer the cells(1,1) by assigning the value 1 to it. During the second iteration the value of i is 2 so it refer the cell(2,1) by assigning the value 2 to it.

Next i –This statement iterate the loop until the final value is reached

Output

	A	B	C	D	E	F
1	1					
2	2					
3	3					
4	4					
5	5					
6	6					
7	7					
8	8					
9	9					
10	10					
11						
12						
13						

Fig 6.2 Output for Fig6.1

6.2 For loop statement with step value

```
Sub forloop()

Dim i As Integer
'For loop
For i = 1 To 10 Step 2
    Sheets(1).Cells(i, 1).Value = i
Next i

End Sub
```

Fig 6.3 For loop with step value

In the previous example the counter value will be increase by 1 after the end of each iteration but in this example the counter value will be increased by 2 after each iteration and the same will be reflect in the statement Sheets(1).Cells(i, 1).Value = i

During the first iteration, the value of i is 1 so it assign the value 1 in cell(1,1) .In the second iteration, counter increased by 2 which means the value of i is 3 (1+2) so it assign the value 3 in the cell(3,1) by skipping the cell(2,1)

Output

	A	B	C	D	E
1	1				
2					
3	3				
4					
5	5				
6					
7	7				
8					
9	9				
10					
11					

Fig 6.4 Output of Fig 6.3

6.3 For statement with Exit For

The practical purpose of the exit for loop is to terminate the iteration when certain condition met. In that case, compiler goes out of for loop without doing any further iteration.

```
Sub forloop()

Dim i As Integer
'For loop with Exit For

For i = 1 To 10

    If i = 7 Then
        Exit For
    End If

    Sheets(1).Cells(i, 1).Value = i

Next i

End Sub
```

Fig 6.5 For statement with Exit For

The above statement iterate the loop until the value of counter i is 7.Once the value of i reaches 7 then **for** loop will be terminated even though its counter end value is 10.

Output

	A	B	C	D
1	1			
2	2			
3	3			
4	4			
5	5			
6	6			
7				
8				
9				
10				

Fig 6.6 Output of Fig 6.5

6.4 Nested For loop

For loop can be nested by putting one or more number of for loop within another for loop but each loop should have different counter variable.

```
Sub forloop()

Dim i As Integer
'Nested For loop

For i = 1 To 10

    For j = 1 To 10

        Sheets(1).Cells(i, j).Value = i + j

    Next j

Next i

End Sub
```

Fig 6.7 Nested For loop

Outer For statement starts iterating with value 1 so compiler goes to inner For statement and iterate with value 1 and execute the statement within the inner for loop.

After the statement executed the inner For loop counter will be increased and iteration continues until the inner For loop reaches its final value 10.

Then control goes out of the inner for loop and increment the counter of the Outer For loop by 2 then it goes on untill the Outer For loop reaches the value 10

Sheets(1).Cells(i, j).Value = i + j

During the execution of the for loop if the iteration value of i is 6 and j is 9 then substitue it to the above statement and the result will be

Sheets(1).Cells(6,9).value=6+9 which means it print the value 15 in the cell(6,9)

Output

	A	B	C	D	E	F	G	H	I	J	K
1	2	3	4	5	6	7	8	9	10	11	
2	3	4	5	6	7	8	9	10	11	12	
3	4	5	6	7	8	9	10	11	12	13	
4	5	6	7	8	9	10	11	12	13	14	
5	6	7	8	9	10	11	12	13	14	15	
6	7	8	9	10	11	12	13	14	15	16	
7	8	9	10	11	12	13	14	15	16	17	
8	9	10	11	12	13	14	15	16	17	18	
9	10	11	12	13	14	15	16	17	18	19	
10	11	12	13	14	15	16	17	18	19	20	
11											
12											
13											
14											
15											
16											

Fig 6.8 Output of Nested For loop

6.5 For Each Next loop

This loop will be useful when you need to process through each element in a collection of elements. The loop iteration depends upon the number of elements present in the collections. For example cell is an element and Range is collection of cells.

Syntax

For Each <element> in <collections>

> *<instructions>*

Next

```
Sub fornext()
Dim a As Range
Set a = Range("A1:B6")

'For each next loop
For Each cell In a
     cell.Value = 2
Next

End Sub
```

Fig 6.9 For each next loop

Beside integer, single as data type VBA also accept Range as a data type. Set command used to assign the given range to the declared variable "a". The purpose of the Set statement is used to convert variable to the object.

If you don't use the set statement VBA will through an error message stating "Object variable or with block variable not set" as shown below

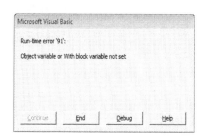

```
Sub fornext()
Dim a As Range

a = Range("A1:B6")

'For each next loop
For Each cell In a
     cell.Value = 2
Next

End Sub
```

Fig 6.10 Object variable Error message

Output

	A	B	C	D
1	2	2		
2	2	2		
3	2	2		
4	2	2		
5	2	2		
6	2	2		
7				
8				
9				

Fig 6.10 Output of Fig 6.9

7)Do Loops

Using the Do loop we can execute the loop as many times as you need until the condition is satisfied or while the condition become true.

There are four different types of Do Loops available in VBA and each has its own unique features.

They are

1)Do Until ..Loop

2)Do while.. Loop

3)DoLoop..Until

4)Do Loop.. while

Now we will see the syntax of all types of Do loop and its examples.

1)Do Until .. Loop

Syntax

Do Until<Condition>

<Instructions>

Loop

Example 7.1

```
Sub doloop()

Dim val As Integer
val = 1

'Do until statements
    Do Until (val = 15)
        Sheets(1).Cells(val, 1) = val + 2
        val = val + 1
    Loop


End Sub
```

Fig 7.1 Do until Loop

In the above example, we declare and initialize variable "val" with value "1".Then, the **Do until** statement begins. This statement compares the value of the variable "val" with 15 and it will iterate the loop until the value is satisfied. We added the counter "**val=val+1**" to increase the value of the variable "val" by 1 after each iteration of the loop.

Do until statement will be executed until the comparison is false. In case if it doesn't met the condition then it turns out to be an infinite loop and it will be executed continuously .

Tip: To cancel the running Macro Press Ctrl+Break

Output

	A	B	C	D	E	F	G
1	3						
2	4						
3	5						
4	6						
5	7						
6	8						
7	9						
8	10						
9	11						
10	12						
11	13						
12	14						
13	15						
14	16						
15							
16							

Fig 7.2 Output of Example 7.1

2) Do Loop Until

The difference between the Do until loop and Do Loop until lies in the condition verification.

In the Do until loop, condition will be verified before the statements in the loop is executed and it will start compiling the statements only after the condition is satisfied otherwise it will exit the Do loop.

In the Do Loop until, statement inside the loop will be executed at least one time even when the condition is failed. Let see the syntax.

Syntax

Do

<Instructions>

Loop Until<Condition>

Example 7.2

```
Sub doloop()

Dim val As Integer
val = 1

'Do loop until statements
    Do
        Sheets(1).Cells(val, 1) = val
        val = val + 1
    Loop Until (val > 15)



End Sub
```

Fig 7.3 Do Loop until

In the above example, when the counter variable "val" reaches 15 condition become failed, because as per the condition the statement should not be executed since 15 is not less than 15. But, it will print the value 15 in the cells(15,1) because the condition is checked only after the Do loop is executed.

Output

	A	B	C	D	E	F	G	H
1	1							
2	2							
3	3							
4	4							
5	5							
6	6							
7	7							
8	8							
9	9							
10	10							
11	11							
12	12							
13	13							
14	14							
15	15							
16								
17								

Fig 7.4Output of Ex 7.2

3)Do While Loop

Do while loop check the condition at initial stage and allow the compiler to compile the statements inside the Do loop only if the condition is true otherwise it skip the Do while loop.

Syntax

Do While<Condition>

<Instructions>

Loop

Example 7.3

```
Sub doloop()
Dim i As Integer
i = 1

'Do while loop

    Do While (i < 20)
        Sheets(1).Cells(i, 2).Value = i
        i = i + 1
    Loop

End Sub
```

Fig 7.5 Do while loop

Do while loop in the above example check condition by comparing the variable "i" with 20 and allow the compiler to execute and print the statements in the cells only if the condition is met and if the condition is false then the loop will be terminated.

Output

	A	B	C	D	E	F	G	
1		1						
2		2						
3		3						
4		4						
5		5						
6		6						
7		7						
8		8						
9		9						
10		10						
11		11						
12		12						
13		13						
14		14						
15		15						
16		16						
17		17						
18		18						
19		19						
20								
21								

Fig 7.6 Do while loop output

4)Do Loop while

The Do loop while statement behave in same way as Do Loop until which means the condition is verified not at the beginning of the loop instead it's done at the end of the loop. So here also, statement inside the loop should be executed at least one time even when the condition fails.

Syntax

Do

<Instructions>

Loop while<condition>

Example 7.4

```
Sub doloop()

Dim i As Integer

i = 9

'Do loop while

    Do
        Sheets(1).Cells(i, 2).Value = i
        i = i + 1
    Loop While (i < 5)

End Sub
```

Fig 7.7 Do Loop while statement

We declare and initialize the variable "i" with value 9. We set the condition for the Do while loop as **(i<5)** so the loop should execute only if (i<5). In our case, it fails because 9 is greater than 5.But the statement will execute and print the value "9" in the cell (9, 2) because as mentioned it will execute at least one entry even the condition is failed.

Output

	A	B	C	D	E
1					
2					
3					
4					
5					
6					
7					
8					
9		9			
10					
11					
12					
13					
14					
15					

Fig 7.8 output of Ex 7.4

5) Do while Loop with Exit Do

Exit Do keyword terminates the Do loop when the condition for the Exit Do is true. This keyword can be used in all the types of Do loops.

Syntax

Do While (Condition)

<Instructions>

Exit Do

Loop

Example 7.5

```
Sub doloop()

Dim i As Integer

i = 1

'Do loop while

    Do While (i < 20)
        Sheets(1).Cells(i, 2).Value = i
        i = i + 1
        If i = 10 Then Exit Do

    Loop

End Sub
```

Fig 7.9 Do while loop with exit do

We set the condition as i=10 if the loop met the condition then the loop will be terminated and no iteration will be executed further even the condition of the do while loop is true.

In the above example the loop should print the value up to i=19 but because of the Exit Do statement it print the value only up to i=9

Output

	A	B	C	D	E	F
1		1				
2		2				
3		3				
4		4				
5		5				
6		6				
7		7				
8		8				
9		9				
10						
11						
12						

Fig 7.10 Output of Ex 7.5

8)Operators in VBA

VBA supports different types of Operators for doing arithmetic calculations, comparisons, concatenations etc. Most commonly used operators in VBA are listed below

1) Arithmetic Operators

2) Comparison Operators

3) Logical Operators

4) Concatenation Operators

When an expression contains more than one operator then VBA has precedence to verify which operator should be executed first. Rules for the order or precedence are

1) Arithmetic operators have higher order of precedence

2) All comparison operators have equal precedence

3) Logical operators have lower order of precedence when compared to arithmetic and comparison Operators

3) Operators with equal precedence will be start executing from left to right

Let us see each of the operators and its purpose in detail

1) Arithmetic Operators

Following are the list of Arithmetic Operators used in VBA

a)^ Operator – Raises number to the power of another number

b)* Operator-Used to multiply the two numbers

c)/ Operator-Used to divide two numbers and return the value in floating point

d)\ Operator-Used to divide two numbers and return the value in integer

e)+ Operator- Used to add two numbers

f)- Operator- Used to subtract two numbers

Example 8.1

```
Sub doloop()
Dim i, j
i = 20
j = 15

'Exponetiation
Dim exp
exp = i ^ 3
Sheets(1).Cells(1, 1).Value = exp

'Multiplication
Dim mul
mul = i * j
Sheets(1).Cells(2, 1).Value = mul

'Division with floating point
Dim divf
divf = i / j
Sheets(1).Cells(3, 1).Value = divf

'Division with integer value
Dim divi
divi = i \ j
Sheets(1).Cells(4, 1).Value = divi

'Addition
Dim add
add = i + j
Sheets(1).Cells(5, 1).Value = add

'Subtraction
Dim subt
subt = i - j
Sheets(1).Cells(5, 1).Value = subt
End Sub
```

Fig 8.1 Arithmetic Operations

The variables i , j declared doesn't have any data type like integer ,double so as already discussed it assume the default data type variant

Exponentiation operator raises the number to the power of another number

Exp i^3 -> Value of "i" is 20 and raised it to three times (20*20*20=800)

Multiplication operator multiply the variable 'i' and 'j' (20*15=300)

Division operator divide the two variable with floating point (20/15=1.333)

Another division operator divide the two variable and return only the integer value even though it return decimal value (20\15=1)

Addition operator add the two variable (20+15=35)

Subtraction operator subtract the value j from i (20-15=5)

In the above example we are doing addition and subtraction in the same cell (5,1) so the latest statement(subtraction) will be executed in the cell.

Output

	A	B	C	D	E
1	8000				
2	300				
3	1.333333				
4	1				
5	5				
6					
7					
8					
9					
10					
11					

Fig 8.2 Output of Ex 8.1

2) Comparison Operator

Syntax

First Variable *Comparision Operator* Second Variable

Following are the list of Comparison operators used in VBA

a) < Operator – Compare the two variables to ensure that first variable is lesser than the second variable

b) <= Operator –Compare the two variables to ensure that first variable is lesser than or equal to the second variable

c) > Operator - Compare the two variables to ensure that first variable is greater than the second variable

d) >=Operator - Compare the two variables to ensure that first variable is greater than or equal to the second variable

e) = Operator – Compare the two variables to ensure that first variable is equal to the second variable

f) <> Operator- Compare the two variables to ensure that first variable is not equal to the second variable

Example 8.2

```
Sub doloop()

Dim i, j, k, l, m
i = 10
j = 15
k = 30
l = 25
m = 15


'< less than operator
If (i < j) Then Sheets(1).Cells(1, 1).Value = "i is less than j"


'<= less than or equal to operator
If (i <= j) Then Sheets(1).Cells(2, 1).Value = "i is lesser than or equal to j"

'> Greater than operator
If (k > l) Then Sheets(1).Cells(3, 1).Value = "k is greater than l"

'>= Greater than or equal to opertor
If (k >= l) Then Sheets(1).Cells(4, 1).Value = "k is greater than or equal to l"

'= equal to operator
If (j = m) Then Sheets(1).Cells(5, 1).Value = "j is equal to m"

'<> Not equal to operator
If (l <> m) Then Sheets(1).Cells(6, 1).Value = "l is not equal to m"


End Sub
```

Fig 8.3 Comparison Operator

If (i < j) Then Sheets(1).Cells(1, 1).Value = "i is less than j"

The above statement compare the value of i with j and its true so it print the statement "i is less than j" in the cell (1,1)

Note: If any of the text is enclosed in "" then VBA consider the text inside the statement as string and print as it is in the corresponding cell

If (i <= j) Then Sheets(1).Cells(2, 1).Value = "i is lesser than or equal to j"

The above statement is also true because 10 is lesser than or equal to 15 so it print the output

If (k > l) Then Sheets(1).Cells(3, 1).Value = "k is greater than l"

The value of k is 30 and l is 25 so definitely 30 is greater than 25 and it also print the output

54

If (k >= l) Then Sheets(1).Cells(4, 1).Value = "k is greater than or equal to l" – this is also true

If (j = m) Then Sheets(1).Cells(5, 1).Value = "j is equal to m"

The value of j is 15 and m is also 15 so both are equal and its print the output

If (l <> m) Then Sheets(1).Cells(6, 1).Value = "l is not equal to m"

The value of l is 25 and m is 15 so both are not equal to each other.

Output

	A	B	C	D
1	i is less than j			
2	i is lesser than or equal to j			
3	k is greater than l			
4	k is greater than or equal to l			
5	j is equal to m			
6	l is not equal to m			
7				
8				
9				
10				

Fig 8.4 Output of Ex 8.2

3) Logical Operator

Following are the list of most commonly used Logical Operator in VBA

a) And operator – Compare two expressions and it set to true only if both are true

b) OR operator- Compare two expressions and it set to true at least if one of the expression is true

c) Not Operator-Evaluate the expressions and if the expression is true then it return false else it return true

Example 8.3

Now, we will slightly modify the Ex 8.2 to understand the logical operator

```
Sub operators()

Dim i, j, k, l, m
i = 10
j = 15
k = 30
l = 25
m = 15

'And operator
If (i < j) And (i <= j) Then Sheets(1).Cells(1, 1).Value = "And operator executed"

'Or operator
If (k > l) Or (k < l) Then Sheets(1).Cells(2, 1).Value = "Or operator executed"

'Not operator
If Not (i = j) Then Sheets(1).Cells(3, 1).Value = "Not operator executed"



End Sub
```

Fig 8.5 Logical Operator

If (i < j) And (i <= j) Then Sheets(1).Cells(1, 1).Value = "And operator executed"

In the above statement both the expressions are true so the AND condition is true.

'Or operator

If (k > l) Or (k < l) Then Sheets(1).Cells(2, 1).Value = "Or operator executed"

In the above statement (k>l) is true & (k<l) is not true but OR operator set to true if any of the one condition is true.

If Not (i = j) Then Sheets(1).Cells(3, 1).Value = "Not operator executed"

We know i value is 10 and j value is 15 and both are not equal so the Not operator is true and the output will be printed

Output

	A	B	C
1	And operator executed		
2	Or operator executed		
3	Not operator executed		
4			
5			
6			
7			
8			
9			
10			

Fig 8.6 Output of Ex 8.3

4) Assignment Operator

Following are the list of most commonly used Assignment Operator

a)& - It is used to combine the strings

b)+ It is also used to concatenate the strings

Example 8.4

	A	B	C	D
1	John	Henry		
2	Bob	Mike		
3	Helen	Peter		
4				
5				
6				
7				

Fig 8.7 Concatenation operator Demo

Now we are going to combine the first name given in the column "A" and second name given in the column "B" and displaying it in the Column "C" using "&" Operator

```
Sub assignop()

Dim fname1, fname2, fname3, lname1, lname2, lname3, fulname1, fulname2, fulname3
fname1 = Sheets(1).Cells(1, 1)
fname2 = Sheets(1).Cells(2, 1)
fname3 = Sheets(1).Cells(3, 1)
lname1 = Sheets(1).Cells(1, 2)
lname2 = Sheets(1).Cells(2, 2)
lname3 = Sheets(1).Cells(3, 2)
'Using the '&' Operator
fulname1 = fname1 & lname1
fulname2 = fname2 & lname2
fulname3 = fname3 & lname3

'Displaying the full name in the column "C"
Sheets(1).Cells(1, 3) = fulname1
Sheets(1).Cells(2, 3) = fulname2
Sheets(1).Cells(3, 3) = fulname3


End Sub
```

Fig 8.8 Concatenation operator

As of now we saw how to assign the value to the cells by using the '=" Operator like Sheets(1).Cells(1,1).value =5

But in the above example we need to get the value from the cells to concatenate. To do that we declared variables such as fname1, fname2 etc. and assign the values in the cells to the variables as shown below

Dim fname1, fname2, fname3, lname1, lname2, lname3, fulname1, fulname2, fulname3

fname1 = Sheets(1).Cells(1, 1)

fname2 = Sheets(1).Cells(2, 1)

fname3 = Sheets(1).Cells(3, 1)

lname1 = Sheets(1).Cells(1, 2)

lname2 = Sheets(1).Cells(2, 2)

lname3 = Sheets(1).Cells(3, 3)

Now all the six names including the first name and last name in the Cells are stored in the variable and we need to combine them using '&' operator and store it in to another variables called fulname1, fulname2, fulname3

fulname1 = fname1 & lname1

fulname2 = fname2 & lname2

fulname3 = fname3 & lname3

Above three statements combine the name and store it in to the corresponding variable but it won't get displayed anywhere in excel sheet. To display the values of the variables in the excel sheet use the below statements

Sheets(1).Cells(1, 3) = fulname1

Sheets(1).Cells(2, 3) = fulname2

Sheets(1).Cells(3, 3) = fulname3

Output

	A	B	C	
1	John	Henry	JohnHenry	
2	Bob	Mike	BobMike	
3	Helen	Peter	HelenPeter	
4				
5				
6				
7				

Fig 8.9 Output of Ex 8.4

The output concatenate the names successfully but we need ',' to separate the first name and last name. Let us see how to do that

Example 8.5

```vba
Sub assignop()

Dim fname1, fname2, fname3, lname1, lname2, lname3, fulname1, fulname2, fulname3
fname1 = Sheets(1).Cells(1, 1)
fname2 = Sheets(1).Cells(2, 1)
fname3 = Sheets(1).Cells(3, 1)
lname1 = Sheets(1).Cells(1, 2)
lname2 = Sheets(1).Cells(2, 2)
lname3 = Sheets(1).Cells(3, 2)
'Using the '&' Operator
fulname1 = fname1 & "," & lname1
fulname2 = fname2 & "," & lname2
fulname3 = fname3 & "," & lname3

'Displaying the full name in the columnt "C"
Sheets(1).Cells(1, 3) = fulname1
Sheets(1).Cells(2, 3) = fulname2
Sheets(1).Cells(3, 3) = fulname3


End Sub
```

Fig 8.10 Concatenation with comma delimiter

We didn't change much just we used two '&' operator and comma enclosed in the quotation i.e. ",".

fulname1 = fname1 & "," & lname1

In the above statement fname& "," results combine the first name and comma and it's finally combined with last name with the help of another '&' operator.

Output

	A	B	C	[
1	John	Henry	John,Henry	
2	Bob	Mike	Bob,Mike	
3	Helen	Peter	Helen,Peter	
4				
5				
6				
7				
o				

Fig 8.11 Output of Ex 8.5

Example 8.6

Concatenation is also possible with the help of '+' Operator.

```
Sub assignop()

Dim fname1, fname2, fname3, lname1, lname2, lname3, fulname1, fulname2, fulname3
fname1 = Sheets(1).Cells(1, 1)
fname2 = Sheets(1).Cells(2, 1)
fname3 = Sheets(1).Cells(3, 1)
lname1 = Sheets(1).Cells(1, 2)
lname2 = Sheets(1).Cells(2, 2)
lname3 = Sheets(1).Cells(3, 2)
'Using the '&' Operator
fulname1 = fname1 + "," + lname1
fulname2 = fname2 + "," + lname2
fulname3 = fname3 + "," + lname3

'Displaying the full name in the column "C"
Sheets(1).Cells(1, 3) = fulname1
Sheets(1).Cells(2, 3) = fulname2
Sheets(1).Cells(3, 3) = fulname3



End Sub
```

Fig 8.12 Concatenation using '+' operator

The '+' operator also does the same thing as '&' Operator when it identified the values stored in the variable as string

Output

	A	B	C	D
1	John	Henry	John,Henry	
2	Bob	Mike	Bob,Mike	
3	Helen	Peter	Helen,Peter	
4				
5				
6				
7				
8				

Fig 8.13 Output of Ex 8.6

Example 8.7

We can able to see the difference between '+' and '&' operator when handling with numeric values. We will use the same Macro but we replaced the first name and last name with some numeric values as shown below

	A	B	C
1	10	13	
2	11	14	
3	12	15	
4			
5			
6			

Fig 8.14 Input for Ex 8.7

Execute the same code as displayed in the Ex 8.4

```
Sub assignop()

Dim fname1, fname2, fname3, lname1, lname2, lname3, fulname1, fulname2, fulname3
fname1 = Sheets(1).Cells(1, 1)
fname2 = Sheets(1).Cells(2, 1)
fname3 = Sheets(1).Cells(3, 1)
lname1 = Sheets(1).Cells(1, 2)
lname2 = Sheets(1).Cells(2, 2)
lname3 = Sheets(1).Cells(3, 2)
'Using the '&' Operator
fulname1 = fname1 & lname1
fulname2 = fname2 & lname2
fulname3 = fname3 & lname3

'Displaying the full name in the columnt "C"
Sheets(1).Cells(1, 3) = fulname1
Sheets(1).Cells(2, 3) = fulname2
Sheets(1).Cells(3, 3) = fulname3


End Sub
```

Fig 8.15 Concatenation operator with integer values

Output

	A	B	C	D
1	10	13	1013	
2	11	14	1114	
3	12	15	1215	
4				
5				
6				
7				

Fig 8.16 Output for Ex 8.7

The concatenation operator '**&**' won't perform any calculation with numeric values it's just assumed numerals as String and concatenate it.

10 and 13 concatenated results in '1013'

Example 8.8

What happens if we use '+' instead of '&' in the above case

```
Sub assignop()

Dim fname1, fname2, fname3, lname1, lname2, lname3, fulname1, fulname2, fulname3
fname1 = Sheets(1).Cells(1, 1)
fname2 = Sheets(1).Cells(2, 1)
fname3 = Sheets(1).Cells(3, 1)
lname1 = Sheets(1).Cells(1, 2)
lname2 = Sheets(1).Cells(2, 2)
lname3 = Sheets(1).Cells(3, 2)
'Using the '&' Operator
fulname1 = fname1 + lname1
fulname2 = fname2 + lname2
fulname3 = fname3 + lname3

'Displaying the full name in the columnt "C"
Sheets(1).Cells(1, 3) = fulname1
Sheets(1).Cells(2, 3) = fulname2
Sheets(1).Cells(3, 3) = fulname3



End Sub
```

Fig 8.17 Concatenation using '+' Operator

Output

	A	B	C	D
1	10	13	23	
2	11	14	25	
3	12	15	27	
4				
5				
6				

Fig8.18 Output of Ex 8.8

The '+' operator behaves in different way when handling with numerals. It added the two columns instead of concatenation. Be aware of using '+' operator for concatenation and it's advisable to use the & operator for concatenation

9) Understanding the VB Editor

Fig 9.1 shows the VB editor screen. It contain three frames Project explorer, Programming window and properties screen.

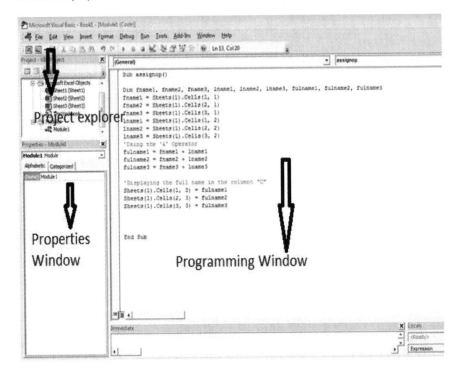

Fig 9.1 VB Editor screen

Project Explorer

The project explorer window display the list of open workbook and its sheets under the Microsoft Excel object, list of modules under the Module tree view, list of class modules under the class modules.

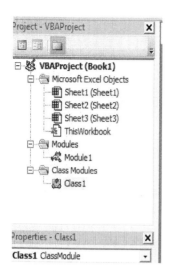

Fig 9.2 Project Explorer

If you need to open sheet 1 then double click the sheet1 in the Microsoft Excel objects and if you need to access the modules under the Modules folder, you can do it by clicking on the available modules in the Module folder.

To display the project explorer window select view->Project Explorer or Ctrl + R

To insert a new module Go to Insert->Module then new module name Module1 will be inserted under the Modules folder. If you want you can change the name of the module in the properties window by clicking on it and changes its name in the Properties window.

To insert a new class Go to Insert->Class then new class named Class1 will be inserted under the class Modules folder as shown in the Fig 9.2

To insert a userform Go to Insert ->Userform then new userform named Userform1 will be inserted under the Forms folder as shown in the Fig 9.3. User form is out of scope of this book.

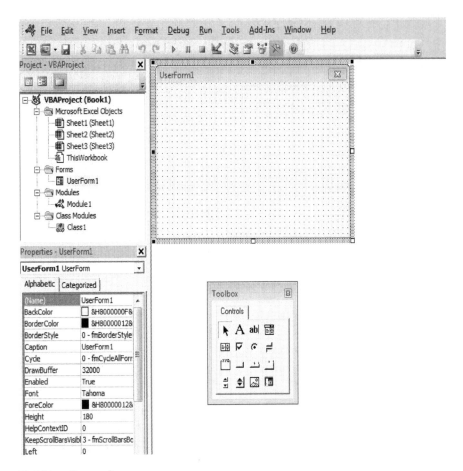

Fig 9.3 Inserting user form

Properties window

It allows the user to edit the properties of various components such as workbook, worksheets, modules and classes. It will list different options according to the components selected. To display the properties window View->Properties window or press F4.Fig 9.4 display the list of properties available for sheet 1

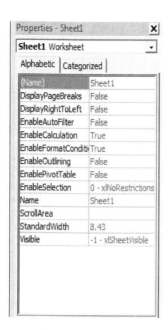

Fig 9.4 Properties window

Programming window

It is the place where we are writing our modules and classes code.

Fig 9.5 Programming window

Object browser

It allows the user to find the objects, properties and methods available in VBA. To view the object browser View ->Object browser or press F2.

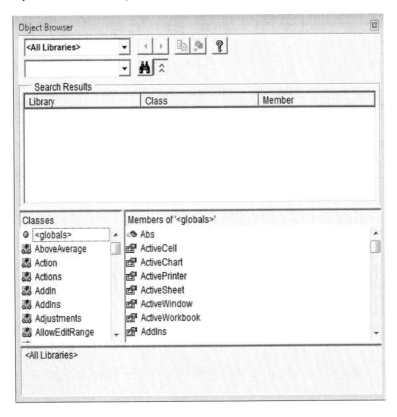

Fig 9.6 Object Browser window

10)Function procedures

Function in VBA is used to perform some functions and return the value.VBA generally allow user to create function procedure and sub procedure. The difference between the function procedure and subprocedure is function procedure return value but sub procedure doesn't return value. To create your own functions or formulas you can go for function procedure. Even though excel has n number of function it also allow the user to create their own functions as well.

Syntax

<Public> or <Private> or <static> Function <functionname> (Argument) as data type

<Instructions>

<Exit function>

<Instructions>

End Function

Public: The public keyword is optional and the purpose of this keyword is to make the function accessible to all the procedures in active VBA

Private: The private keyword is optional and the purpose of this keyword is to make the function accessible only to the procedures available in the module where function exist and other modules and procedures are not able to access the private function

Static: This keyword is also optional and it indicate that the variable declared in the functions are preserved

Function: using this statement compiler understand that function procedure begins

Function name: Here you have to mention your function name and the rules for the function name is same as variable name rules

Argument: Arguments are the input parameter to the function procedures

Data type: This determine the type of data returned by the function like string, integer

Instructions: This indicate the statement you want to happen in your function

Exit Functions: It terminate the execution of function before it ends

End Function: It indicate the end of the function

Example 10.1

Now we will create a function to calculate the area of rectangle and for that we need two parameter length and breadth.

We need to get the length and breadth from user and multiply it and return the value.

```
Function AreaRect(length As Integer, breadth As Integer) As Integer

AreaRect = length * breadth


End Function
```

Fig 10.1 Function for Area of rectangle

The name of the function is AreaRect and to access the function in excel you need to enter its name followed by two parameter length and breadth. Then excel will display the result

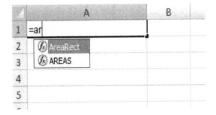

Fig 10.2 Accessing the function

Accessing our own function is similar to accessing other in-built functions in excel as demonstrated in the Fig 10.2

	A	B	C	D
1	Length	Breadth	Area	
2	15	36	=AreaRect(A2,B2)	
3	34	56		
4	45	63		
5				
6				
7				
8				
9				

Fig 10.3 Area of Rectangle function

For the function you can give the input parameter as value of another cell and when you press "Enter" it display the value of Rectangle Area and we can use the same formula anywhere in the workbook.

	A	B	C	D
1	Length	Breadth	Area	
2	15	36	540	
3	34	56	1904	
4	45	63	2835	
5				
6				
7				
8				

Fig 10.4 Output of functions

Calling the function from sub procedure

VBA allow user to call the functions in Sub procedure code too but the sub procedure should lies in the module where function procedure exist if the access of the function is private

Now let us take the same input but we are executing it through sub procedure. Before executing the code the excel sheet should be as show in the Fig 10.5

	A	B	C	I
1	Length	Breadth	Area	
2	15	36		
3	34	56		
4	45	63		
5				
6				

Fig 10.5 Input for sub procedure

Using for loop we start iteration from second row to fourth row. Then we are passing the input parameter to the functions by specifying the cell position like sheets(1).cells(1,1) and assign the output returned by the function to the respective cell using the "=" assignment operator

Sheets(1).Cells(i, 3) = AreaRect(Sheets(1).Cells(i, 1), Sheets(1).Cells(i, 2))

```
Sub areacalc()

For i = 2 To 4
Sheets(1).Cells(i, 3) = AreaRect(Sheets(1).Cells(i, 1), Sheets(1).Cells(i, 2))
Next i

End Sub
```

```
Function AreaRect(length As Integer, breadth As Integer) As Integer


AreaRect = length * breadth



End Function
```

Fig 10.6 Calling function with sub procedure

Click F5 to execute. It display the output as shown in the Fig 10.7

	A	B	C	D
1	Length	Breadth	Area	
2	15	36	540	
3	34	56	1904	
4	45	63	2835	
5				
6				
7				

Fig 10.7 Output

11)MsgBox and InputBox Functions

1)MsgBox Function

It is very helpful if you need to show any message like warning sign, prompting or caution to the user.VBA allow you to display your error message in different styles which suits your need. It is one of the most commonly used functions in VBA so you must get familiar with this function.

Syntax

Msgbox(Prompt,[Button Style],[Title])

Prompt: It display the text given in the parameter to the Message box text

Button: It specifies what buttons to be available on the MsgBox(Optional)

Title: It specifies the title of the MsgBox(Optional)

The main purpose of the msgbox function is to display a message to the user and prompt the user to click on button shown in the screen.

There are different button styles available in VBA. Most commonly used styles are

Value	Constant	Description
0	vbOkOnly	Ok button
1	vbOkCancel	ok and Cancel button
2	VbAbortRetryIgnore	Abort, Retry and Ignore button
3	VbYesNoCancel	Yes,No and Cancel button
4	VbYesNo	Yes and No button
5	vbRetryCancel	Retry and Cancel button
16	vbCritical	Critical icon
32	vbQuestion	Warning query icon
48	vbExclamation	warning message icon
64	vbInformation	Information message icon

Simple Msgbox function

Let us ask the user "How are you?" with the help of msgbox function.

```
Sub msgboxfun()

 MsgBox "Hello how are you?"

End Sub
```

Fig 11.1 Simple Msgbox function

Fig 11.1 contain statement MsgBox "Hello how are you?" and we gave only one argument
"Hello how are you?" so the msgbox by default understood the argument as prompt message
and display the text in the pop up box, set the default title as "Microsoft Excel" with OK button
as shown in the below Fig 11.2

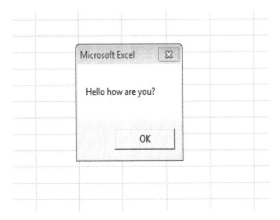

Fig 11.2 Simple Msgbox

Specifying Parameter by Position

If you want to make the msgbox by specifying its position then you need to make sure that you
gave the parameters in the correct order.

```
Sub msgboxfun()

 MsgBox "Something is burning", vbCritical + vbOKCancel, "Alert"

End Sub
```

Fig 11.3 Specifying parameter by position

"Something is burning"->This is identified as message text by the compiler since its parameterized in the first position

vbCritical+vbOkCancel- VBA allow user to combine the button and icon but you cannot combine icon and icon and button and button. It's identified as button or icon since it's mentioned in the second position.

"Alert" –VBA identified as Title since it's mentioned in the third position.

VBA identify the parameter with the help of delimiter comma. The output of the Fig 11.3 is shown below

Fig 11.4 Output of Fig 11.4

Specifying Parameter by name

The advantage of specifying the parameter by name is

1) Its appear more readable to the user

2) You don't need to follow the order (prompt, button, title) you are allowed to specify any parameter anywhere

To specify the parameter by name then you need to separate its title and value by ":="

Syntax

MsgBox Prompt:="Your text message",Buttons:=vbOKCancel + vbInformation, Title:="Your title"

```
Sub msgboxfun()

  MsgBox Prompt:="Are you ready", Title:="Come on", Buttons:=vbOKCancel + vbInformation


End Sub
```

Fig 11.5 Msgbox by name

In the Fig 11.5 I changed the order by mentioning title first rather than button but it as I said before it doesn't work by position instead it work by name

Fig 11.6 Output of Fig 11.5

Specifying button name by constant

VBA allow user to specify the buttons not only by name but also by constants assigned to each type of buttons. Let's see one instance of it by replacing the Fig 11.5 by constant instead of name.

```
Sub msgboxfun()

  MsgBox Prompt:="Are you ready", Title:="Come on", _
  Buttons:=1 + 64

End Sub
```

Fig 11.7 Specifying button by constant

I replaced the vbOkCancel+vbInformation by 1+64 but it does display the same output. As well you need to notice one more thing I used a special character underscore '_' in-between the title and buttons. *If your statement is long or you want to skip the statement to the next line for your own reference then you can use Underscore.*

Fig 11.8 Output for Fig 11.7

You have to follow the below rules to skip the statement to next line.

-After reaching the end of the first statement you have to give space and then use underscore otherwise compiler will through error message. If you didn't gave space you will get the error as shown in the Fig 11.8

```
Sub msgboxfun()

    MsgBox Prompt:="Are you ready", Title:="Come on",_
    Buttons:=1 + 64

End Sub
```

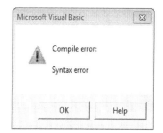

Fig 11.9 Error message

-You cannot use the underscore inside the double quotations as shown in Fig 11.9

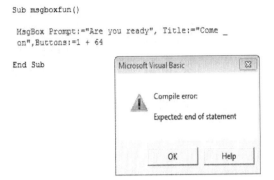

```
Sub msgboxfun()

  MsgBox Prompt:="Are you ready", Title:="Come _
  on",Buttons:=1 + 64

End Sub
```

Fig 11.10 Error message for using underscore in between the double quotations.

Input returned by User

We are familiar with making msgbox with styles, title and buttons but how would you know what button is chosen by the user to process the task?

You can get the button clicked by the user once you assign the msgbox function to the variable and comparing the variable name with button constant.

```
Sub msgboxfun()

Dim msg
msg = MsgBox(Prompt:="Are you ready", Title:="Come on", _
 Buttons:=vbYesNoCancel)

'Getting the button clicked by the user
If msg = vbYes Then
Sheets(1).Cells(1, 1).Value = "Yes Im ready :)"
ElseIf msg = vbNo Then
Sheets(1).Cells(1, 1).Value = "No I need some time to get ready :("
Else
Sheets(1).Cells(1, 1).Value = "Im not sure :P"
End If

End Sub
```

Fig 11.11 Getting input from the user

We declared a variable name 'msg' and assign the variable to the msgbox function. When you are assigning a msgbox function to any of the variable then you need to enclose its parameters by angular brackets as shown in the Fig 11.10.

To get the input chosen by the user we need to assign variable to buttons used in the msgbox function using if else statement or select case statement as you need.

If the user chosen the "Yes" button then it will print the text "Yes I'm ready" in the cell(1,1) or if the user chosen the "No" button then it will print the text "No I need some time to get ready" in the cell(1,1) or if the user doesn't choose yes or no button then by default compiler understood that "cancel" button is chosen by the user and display the text "I'm not sure" in the cell(1,1).I will go with "Yes" and its output is shown in the Fig 11.12

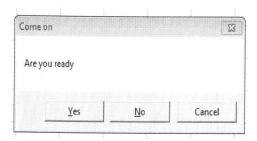

Fig 11.12 Msgbox to get input from the user

Output

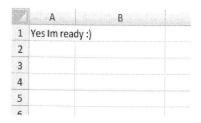

Fig 11.13 Output for Fig 11.10

InputBox Function

This is a most commonly used function to get the input from the user by displaying the prompt message box with title ,with Ok and Cancel buttons.

Syntax

InputBox (Title, prompt, Defaulttext, X-position, Y-psostion)

Title-Input given in the parameter is displayed as Title name

Prompt-Input given in the parameter is displayed as Text message

Default Text-Display the text to be displayed in the user input box(Optional)

X-Position-Specify the X-Coordinate(optional)

Y-Position-Specify the Y-coordinate(Optional)

You can specify the parameters by its name or its position as mentioned in the msgbox function.

Let us see an example with InputBox function

```
Sub msgboxfun()

Dim inp As String

inp = InputBox(Prompt:="Enter your sex 'M' or 'F' ", Title:="Gender", Default:= _
"M or F")


If inp = "M" Then
Sheets(1).Cells(1, 1).Value = "Im a Male "
ElseIf inp = "F" Then
Sheets(1).Cells(1, 1).Value = "Im a Female"
Else
Sheets(1).Cells(1, 1).Value = "Im a Shemale"
End If

End Sub
```

Fig 11.14 InputBox function

Input box behave in the same way as message box function. We are declared a variable and assign the variable to the input box function to get the input given by the user. When user Run the above command it will display the InputBox as shown in Fig 11.14

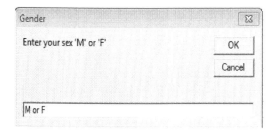

Fig 11.15 Input box displayed

When user edit the text box and enter M and click the OK button then it will print the output in cells (1,1) as shown in Fig 11.15

Fig 11.16 Output of InputBox function

12) String Functions

VBA provides functions more than the user expectations for handling the strings. String is a sequence of characters containing numerals, words and special characters. We will see the list of most commonly used functions to handle the strings.

1)InStr

2)Left

3)Right

4)Mid

5)Lcase

6)Ucase

7)Len

8)Ltrim

9)Rtrim

10)Trim

11)InstrRev

12)Space

Let us see each of functions in detail

1)Instr

It return an integer which specifying the first occurrence of the sub string in the main string starting from the first position

Syntax

Instr([start], string, substring,[compare])

Start-It indicates the starting position for the search and it should be an integer value. If the parameter is omitted search start from the 1st position.(Optional)

String-It is the main string where you need to start your search

Substing-It represents the string you need to find within the main string

Compare-It specify the type of comparison (Optional)

Below are the main string in the cells(1,1)

	A	B
1	Set of characters grouping together to form a string.we are considering this as main string for study purpose.We are now going to play with all the string functions using this text.	
2		
3		

Fig 12.1 Strings in the cells(1,1)

Using the InStr function now we are going to find the position of the first occurrence of the substring "to" within the main string.

```
Sub strings()

Dim str As String, substr As String, pos As Integer

str = Sheets(1).Cells(1, 1)
substr = "to"
pos = InStr(1, str, substr)
MsgBox "Posistion of the substring'to' is " & pos, vbOKOnly, "String functions"


End Sub
```

Fig 12.2 Instr example

We declared three variables to store the value of substring, main string and position. Initially we assign the strings in the cell (1,1) to the variable "str" ,string we need to find 'to' inside the main string to the variable "substr" and position of the occurrence to the variable "pos".

pos = InStr(1, str, substr)

The above statement starts searching the substring "to" within the main string from the position1 and store the value in the variable "pos".

MsgBox "Position of the substring'to' is " &pos, vbOKOnly, "String functions"

Using the msgbox function we are displaying the position of the substring.

85

The Instr function start finding the first occurrence of the string "to" in the main string and when we take a look at the main string its present inside the word "**to**gether" so it return the position of the letter 't' from the starting position. The output is shown in the Fig 12.3

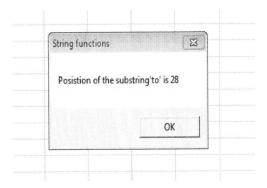

Fig 12.3 Output of Instr function

2)Left

It is used to extract a substring with specified number of characters from main string starting from the left.

Syntax

Left(text,[number of characters])

Text-It represent the main string where you need to extract the sub string

Number of characters-It represents the number of characters you need from the main string starting from the left. If its omitted then it return only one character.(Optional)

Let us see how to extract 7 characters from the Fig 12.1

While extracting, the left function consider the space as a character and return the output.

```
Sub strings()

Dim str As String, substr As String

str = Sheets(1).Cells(1, 1)
substr = Left(str, 7)
MsgBox "Output of Left string function is  " & substr, vbOKOnly, "String functions"


End Sub
```

Fig 12.4 Left functions

Left(str,7)- This statement return the text containing 7 characters as shown in the Fig 12.5 including spaces

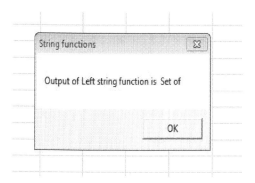

Fig 12.5 Output of Left function

3)Right

It is used to extract a substring with specified number of characters from main string starting from the end of the string.

Syntax

Right(text ,number or character)

Text-It specify the text you want to search within main string

Number of character-It represent the number of characters you need starting from the right string. If it's omitted then it return only one character (Optional).

Let us see how to extract 10 letters starting from the end of the string as shown in the Fig 12.1.

```
Sub strings()

Dim str As String, substr As String
str = Sheets(1).Cells(1, 1).Value
substr = Right(str, 10)
MsgBox "The text extracted is -" & substr, vbOKOnly, "String functions"

End Sub
```

Fig 12.6 Right functions

Right(str,10)- This statement return the 10 characters starting from the end of the main string. The output is shown in the Fig 12.7

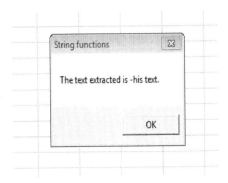

Fig 12.7 Output of Right function

4)Mid

It returns the string with specified number of characters indicated in the parameter anywhere in the middle of the string

Syntax

Mid(text, start position, number of character)

Text- It represents the string you need to extract from the main string

Start position- It should be numerical value. Using this value compiler left off the character from the sub string and returns the remaining characters.

Number of character-It indicates the number character to be returned and if it's omitted then it return the remaining character after the start position.

For e.g.

Main string –"You are learning VBA"

Mid("You are learning",5,6)-This statement find the 5th character in the main string and return 6 character starting from the 5th position so the output will be "are le"

Mid("You are learning VBA,7)- This statement find the 7th character in the main string and return the remaining characters starting from the 7th character. The output will be " learning VBA"

Let us see an example

```
Sub strings()

Dim str As String, substr As String
str = Sheets(1).Cells(1, 1).Value
substr = Mid(str, 10, 15)
MsgBox "The text extracted is -" & substr, vbOKOnly, "String functions"

End Sub
```

Fig 12.8 Mid function

It finds the character in the 10th position and returns 15 characters from the 10th position. The output is shown in the Fig 12.9

Fig 12.9 Output of Mid function

5)Lcase

This function is used to convert all the alphabets to lowercase letters.

Syntax

Lcase(text)

Text-It represents the string which you need to convert to lower case

Example

```
Sub strings()

Dim str As String, substr As String
str = "Hello PeOple ! GooD MoRninG tO EverYoNe"
substr = LCase(str)
MsgBox "The converted lower cases are -" & substr, vbOKOnly, "String functions"

End Sub
```

Fig 12.10 Lcase functions

In the above example, we are providing the input text in the variable str and converted lower case output in the variable substr. Let us see how the output will be

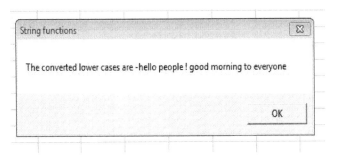

Fig 12.11 Lcase output

6)UCase

It converts all the alphabets to Upper case letters unlike Lcase

Syntax

Ucase(text)

Text-It represents the string which you need to convert to upper case

Let see what happens if Lcase is changed to Ucase in the Fig 12.10

```
Sub strings()

Dim str As String, substr As String
str = "Hello PeOple ! GooD MoRninG tO EverYoNe"
substr = UCase(str)
MsgBox "The converted uppper cases are -" & substr, vbOKOnly, "String functions"

End Sub
```

Fig 12.12 Ucase functions

In the output msgbox function it will convert all the lowercase to upper case letters.

Fig 12.13 Output of Ucase

7)Len

This function returns the length or number of character in the string.

Syntax

Len(text)

Text-It specifies the text you need to know the number of characters in it.

We will see an example

```
Sub strings()

Dim str As String, substr As String
str = "Hello PeOple ! GooD MoRninG tO EverYoNe"
substr = Len(str)

MsgBox "The length of the string is" & substr, _
vbOKOnly, "String functions"

End Sub
```

Fig 12.14 Len function

In the above example, we assign the given text to the variable str and the Len function to the variable substr to return the number of characters in it. Msgbox function return the number of characters including spaces stored in the string str.

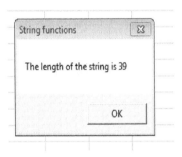

Fig 12.15 Output of Len function

8)Ltrim

This function is used to remove the leading spaces of the string.

Syntax

Ltrim(text)

Text-It indicate the specified string where you need to remove the spaces in the start of the string

Let us see an example

```
Sub strings()

Dim str As String, substr As String
str = "            Hello PeOple ! GooD MoRninG tO EverYoNe"

substr = LTrim(str)

MsgBox "After the leading spaces are removed then string will be" _
& substr, _
vbOKOnly, "String functions"

End Sub
```

Fig 12.16 Ltrim function

When you look at the string stored in the variable **str** you can able to see leading spaces exist before the word "Hello".

After using the ltrim function it will remove the leading spaces in the string but it won't remove the trailing spaces if any.

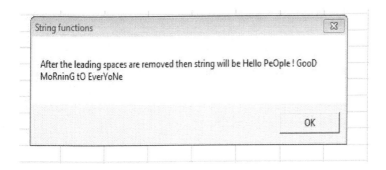

Fig 12.17 Output of Ltrim function

In the above Fig 12.17, you can't find the leading spaces in the string because it was removed by the Ltrim function.

9)Rtrim

It is used to remove the trailing spaces exist in the string

Syntax

Rtrim(text)

Text-It specifies the string where you need to remove the spaces in the trailing edge.

Let us see an example

```
Sub strings()

Dim str As String, substr As String
str = "Hello PeOple ! GooD MoRninG tO EverYoNe          "

substr = RTrim(str)

MsgBox "After the leading spaces are removed then string will be " _
& substr, _
vbOKOnly, "String functions"

End Sub
```

Fig 12.18 Rtrim function

Text stored in the variable str, you can able to find more spaces at the trailing or end of the string. We are removing the spaces with the help of Rtrim function. The output of the Rtrim function is shown in the Fig 12.19

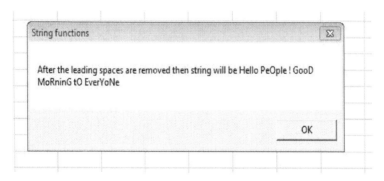

Fig 12.19 Output of Rtrim function

10)Trim

This function is used to remove both the leading and trailing spaces in the string

Syntax

Trim (text)

94

Text- It specify the text where you need to remove the both the leading and trailing spaces in the string

Let us see an example

```
Sub strings()

Dim str As String, substr As String
'More spaces in the start and end of the string

str = "   Hello PeOple ! GooD MoRninG tO EverYoNe        "

substr = RTrim(str)

MsgBox "After the leading spaces are removed then string will be " _
& substr, _
vbOKOnly, "String functions"

End Sub
```

Fig 12.20 Trim function

The string str = " Hello PeOple !GooDMoRninGtOEverYoNe   " contain more spaces in the start and end position of the string. Trim function remove both leading and trailing spaces and return the text without spaces in the leading and trailing. The output of the Trim function is shown in the Fig 12.21

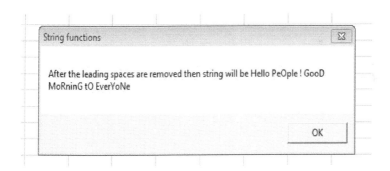

Fig 12.21 Output of Trim function

Note: The spaces between the words "be" and "Hello" is inserted by the msgbox function not by the Trim function.

11)InstrRev

This function is same as Instr but the only difference is it returns the position of the first occurrence of the sub string starting from the end of the string.

Syntax

InStrRev (string,substring,[start],[compare])

String-It specify the main string where you need to perform your search to get the position of string you need

Substring-It specify the string you need to search within main string

Start-It specifies the starting position for your search. If you omitted it will start search from the last character in the main string

Compare-It specify the type of comparison you need to perform.(Not much useful)

```
Sub strings()

Dim pos As Integer

pos = InStrRev("hello where are you", "o")

MsgBox "The positon of word is " _
& pos, _
vbOKOnly, "String functions"

End Sub
```

Fig 12.22 InstrRev Functions

In the above statement, we are trying to find the position of the character 'o' from the end. We are having two 'o' one in the word "hell**o**" and another one in the word "y**o**u". The compiler will start search from the end and return the position (count start from left to right).So it will return the position of the character 'o' in the word 'you' .The output is shown in the Fig 12.22

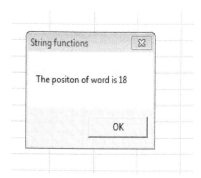

Fig 12.23 Output of InstrRev function

12) Space

It is used to insert the number of spaces as specified by the user.

Syntax

Space (number)

Number-It indicates the number of spaces to be inserted.

Let see an example

```
Sub strings()

Dim str As String

str = Space(50)
num = Len(str)
MsgBox "The number of spaces inserted is   " _
& num, _
vbOKOnly, "String functions"

End Sub
```

Fig 12.24 Space function

We cannot able to see the spaces in the msgbox function, Here, I inserted 50 spaces and counting the number of spaces using Len function and return the output in the msgbox function. The output is shown in the Fig 12.25

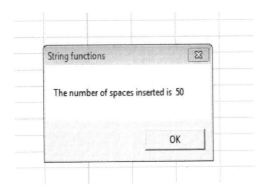

Fig 12.25 Output of Space function

13)Information functions

Information functions return info about the VBA environment. In few cases we need to know, whether the value is date or numeric or blank or text etc. This information function will comes in handy when you need to know such kind of information. Most of the information functions start with "Is" and self-explanatory. We will see the list of information functions, which are very useful for our day to day work.

1)IsNull

2)IsDate

3)IsNumeric

4)IsEmpty

1)IsNull

This function is used to check whether the expression contain valid data or not. If the value or expression is null then it return true otherwise it return false.

Syntax

IsNull(Expression)

Expression-It represents a variant containing string expression or Numeric expression or Null.

Let see an example

```
Sub infofunc()

Dim val

val = Null

    If IsNull(val) Then
    MsgBox "The value of the expression is null", vbOKOnly, "IsNull?"
    Else
    MsgBox "The value of expression is not Null", vbOKOnly, "IsNull?"
    End If

End Sub
```

Fig 13.1 IsNull function

In the Fig 11.1 we declared a variable called "val" and assign the value to "Null" value. Then we verify whether it's null or not with the help of IsNull function. Since the Null value is assigned to variable, it return true. This function will be helpful when you create an object and release it by assigning it to NULL when it purpose ends. The output is shown in the Fig 11.2

Fig 13.2 Output of IsNull Function

When valid data is assigned to the variable then IsNull return the False.

```
Sub infofunc()

Dim val

val = "Hello"

    If IsNull(val) Then
    MsgBox "The value of the expression is null", vbOKOnly, "IsNull?"
    Else
    MsgBox "The value of expression is not Null", vbOKOnly, "IsNull?"
    End If


End Sub
```

Fig 13.3 Is Null Function

In the above macro, the string "Hello" is assigned to variable "val" so definitely it's not Null. So, IsNull function return false. The output is shown in the Fig 11.4

Fig 13.4 Output of Isnull function

2)IsDate

This function used to determine whether the expression is recognized as valid date or time.

Syntax

IsDate (expression)

Expression-It represents a variant containing string expression or date expression or time expression.

Let us evaluate the values in the below Fig 11.5 and determine is it date or not.

	A	B	C	D
1	S.No	Input data	Output	
2	1	5/28/2013		
3	2	19-May-13		
4	3	13/32/2014		
5	4	03.21.10		
6	5	03.22.2024		
7				
8				

Fig 13.5 IsDate Function

The given date and its format is described below

05/28/2013- It represent date in MM/DD/YYYY format

19-May-13-It represents date in DD-Month-YY format

13/32/2014-It represent Invalid date

03.21.10-It represents time in HH:MM:SS format

03.22.1024-It represent invalid time format

```
Sub infofunc()

For i = 2 To 6

If IsDate(Sheets(1).Cells(i, 2).Value) Then
    Sheets(1).Cells(i, 3) = True
Else
    Sheets(1).Cells(i, 3) = False
End If

Next i


End Sub
```

Fig 13.6 Isdate function

Using the for loop we iterate from row 2 to 6.Passing the input data to the IsDate function and if its return true then it enter value "True" in the column 3.If its return false then it enter value "False" in the column 3 corresponding to its input data.

Run the above macro and let us see the output in the Fig 11.7

	A	B	C	D
1	S.No	Input data	Output	
2	1	5/28/2013	TRUE	
3	2	19-May-13	TRUE	
4	3	13/32/2014	FALSE	
5	4	03.21.10	TRUE	
6	5	03.22.2024	FALSE	
7				
8				

Fig 13.7 Output of Is Date function

3)IsNumeric

This function is used to determine whether the expression contain only numeric or not.

Syntax

IsNumeric(Expression)

Expression-It represents variant containing numeric expressions or string expressions or combination of both.

We will prepare an input data for this and evaluate it.

	A	B	C	D
1	S.No	Input data	Output	
2	1	123eraa		
3	2	12.23		
4	3	9995.666		
5	4	90		
6	5	Help 108		
7				

Fig 13.8 IsNumeric function input

```
Sub infofunc()

For i = 2 To 6

If IsNumeric(Sheets(1).Cells(i, 2).Value) Then
    Sheets(1).Cells(i, 3) = True
Else
    Sheets(1).Cells(i, 3) = False
End If

Next i


End Sub
```

Fig 13.9 IsNumeric function

IsNumeric function compare the values are return true if expression contain only numeric value else it return false.

	A	B	C	D	E
1	S.No	Input data	Output		
2	1	123eraa	FALSE		
3	2	12.23	TRUE		
4	3	9995.666	TRUE		
5	4	90	TRUE		
6	5	Help 108	FALSE		
7					

Fig 13.10 Output of IsNumeric Function

4)IsEmpty

This function is used to determine whether the expression or variable is initialized or not.

Syntax

IsEmpty(Expression)

Expression-It represents a variant containing numeric or string or empty.

If the variable is not initialized then the Isempty function returns true but the IsNull function doesn't return true.

```
Sub infofunc()

Dim val1, val2

If IsEmpty(val1) Then
  Sheets(1).Cells(1, 1).Value = "Val1 is empty"
Else
   Sheets(1).Cells(1, 1).Value = "Val1 is not empty"
End If

If IsNull(val2) Then
    Sheets(1).Cells(2, 1).Value = "val2 is Null"
Else
    Sheets(1).Cells(2, 1).Value = "Val2 is not Null"
End If


End Sub
```

Fig 13.11 IsEmpty function

In the above macro, we declared two variable "val1" and "val2" but we didn't initialize the variable with values.

Using IsEmpty function we are determining is it empty or not? Yes it's empty

Using IsNull function we are determining is it null or not? No it's not Null.

	A	B
1	Val1 is empty	
2	Val2 is not empty	
3		
4		
5		

Fig 13.12 Output of Fig 11.11

14) Working with Internet Explorer

VBA allow user to open webpage, extract data from the webpage, and pass data to the webpage with the help of Internet explorer. You can control the components in the webpage such as textbox, button, check box, and drop down box by accessing its html elements. Automating Internet explorer with the help of VBA is very vast subject. I will give an insight about how to do this. But you need to explore yourself much more.

By two ways you can create internet explorer object. They are

1)Late Binding

2)Early Binding

Let see each in detail:

1)Early Binding

This method finds the Internet explorer object with the help of references. To get the reference window dialog box go to Tools ->References. Once the dialog box is opened you need to add two references

 1)Microsoft Internet controls

2)Microsoft HTML object Library

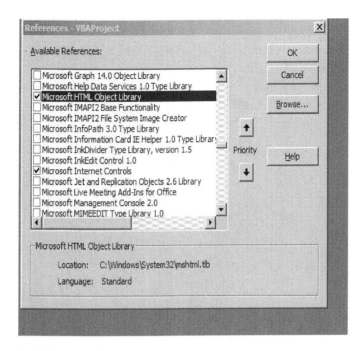

Fig 14.1 Reference Dialog box

2) Late Binding

This method create Internet explorer object at the run time with the help of Object Data type. It's your wish to use any of the method as you need. For late binding you need to create a variable with object data type and set the variable to the create object method. For example

Dim ie as object

Set ie= CreateObject("InternetExplorer.Application)

Let us see how to open Google webpage in the Internet Explorer with the help of VBA(Early Binding)

As I previously mentioned, you need to add the references for Internet explorer automation. After adding the references, you can execute the below macro to open Google webpage

```
Sub ieauto()

Dim ie As InternetExplorer
Set ie = New InternetExplorer

ie.Visible = True
ie.navigate ("https://www.google.com")

Do While ie.Busy
DoEvents
Loop

Do While ie.readyState <> READYSTATE_COMPLETE
DoEvents
Loop


ie.Quit


End Sub
```

Fig 14.2 Automating IE using early Binding

The first statement Dim ie as Internet Explorer declare a variable ie with data type as Internet explorer. We set the variable to new object internet explorer with the help of Set statements.

ie.visible- This denote the visibility of Internet explorer. If it true then you can able to view the internet explorer in the window and if its false it will run in the invisible mode.

ie.navigate("www.google.com)- It took the user to the url given.

Do While ie.Busy

DoEvents

Loop

The above statement keep the code waiting while ie is busy by doing events.

Do While ie.readyState<> READYSTATE_COMPLETE

DoEvents

Loop

The above statement keeps the IE wait until the google webpage is fully loaded.

ie.Quit- It quit the Internet explorer

The output is shown in the Fig 12.3

```
Sub ieauto()

Dim ie As InternetExplorer
Set ie = New InternetExplorer

ie.Visible = True
ie.navigate ("https://www.google.com")

Do While ie.Busy
DoEvents
Loop

Do While ie.readyState <> READYSTATE_COMPLETE
DoEvents
Loop
```

Fig 14.3 Output of IE automation

We can able to access the object like check box, button, drop down box etc. with the help of Html elements. We need to identify its element first before doing automation. There are several methods available in VBA for accessing the elements by ID, tagname, class name etc. But for that you should be somewhat familiar with HTML language.

Let us enter a text in the Google search box button and click on Ok. For that we need to identify two elements 1) Text box element name or ID 2) Google search Button name or ID

Fig 14.4 Google webpage

To identify the element right click on the Internet explorer and click on View Source to view the source code of the Google webpage.

Fig 14.5 To view the source code

A new window will appear with source code

Fig 14.6 Source code of Google webpage

You need to identify the Google text box and search button in the above Fig 12.5.You can use Mozilla firefeox inspect element function to find easily when compared to Internet explorer.

I identified the html elements

For Google search text box, the html element name is "q"

For Google search button, the html element name is "btnK"

Let us enter a word "Cheese" in the Google search text box and click on Search button with the help of VBA.

We can do that either by early binding or Late Binding as you wish.

```
Sub ieauto()

Dim ie As InternetExplorer
Set ie = New InternetExplorer

ie.Visible = True
ie.navigate ("https://www.google.com")

Do While ie.Busy
DoEvents
Loop


Do While ie.readyState <> READYSTATE_COMPLETE
DoEvents
Loop

ie.document.getElementById("lst-ib").Value = "Cheese"

ie.document.getElementById("btnK").Click

Do While ie.Busy
DoEvents
Loop

Do While ie.readyState <> READYSTATE_COMPLETE
DoEvents
Loop

ie.Quit


End Sub
```

Fig 14.7 Accessing the Google webpage

ie.document.getelementByID- This statement find the html elements of the Google text box and search button

Click- This method simulate the click event

ie.quit- It close the Internet explorer

*****

113

Conclusion

Thank you for reading this book. I hope this book definitely help the beginners to step up their programming knowledge. I feel honored to share the knowledge with my readers. I put all my effort to narrate this book in simple, easy and elegant way so that beginners can understand and grasp the content easily. Extensive care has been taken to provide quality content in the book without any grammatical errors and typo errors. If you noticed any errors, please bring to my attention by writing your queries at erajanraja24@gmail.com. I'll put all my effort to correct it as soon as possible.

I have small request for you –Please leave a review for my book and feel free to tell your opinion and suggestions so that it will definitely helpful for me as well as other readers.

Regards

Rajan

Made in the USA
Middletown, DE
24 July 2016